Talking about

Bullying

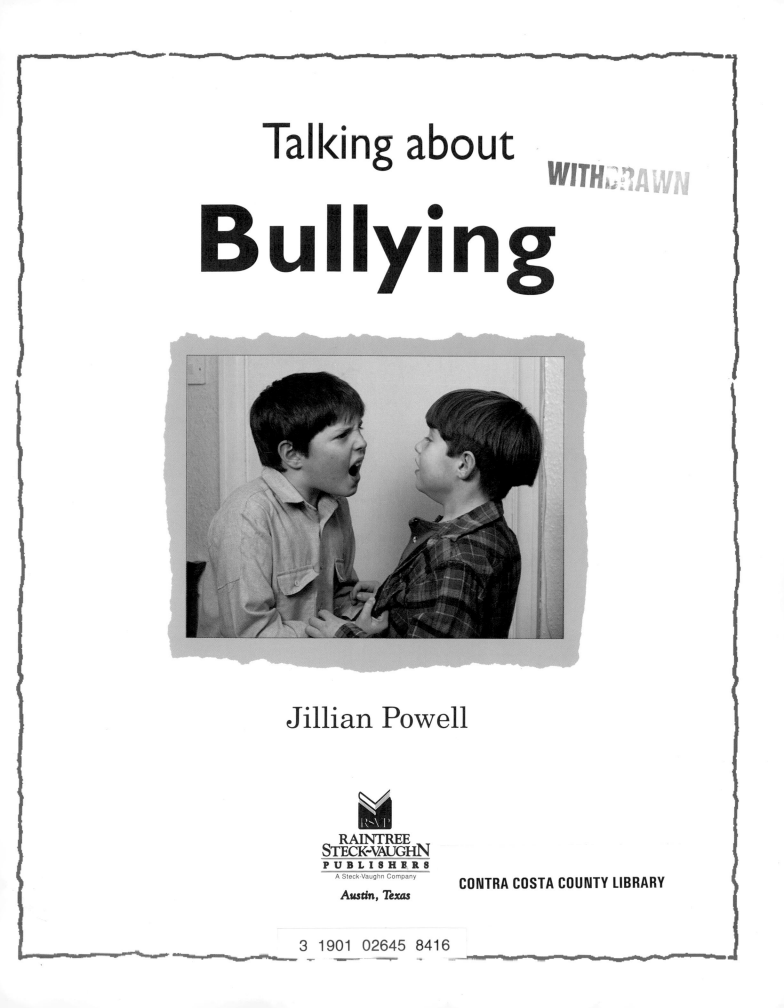

Jillian Powell

RAINTREE
STECK-VAUGHN
PUBLISHERS
A Steck-Vaughn Company

Austin, Texas

Titles in the series
Talking about
Alcohol   **Disability**
Bullying   **Drugs**
Death   **Family Breakup**

Published by Raintree Steck-Vaughn Publishers,
an imprint of Steck-Vaughn Company

Library of Congress Cataloging-in-Publication Data
Powell, Jillian.
Talking about bullying / Jillian Powell.
    p.   cm.—(Talking about)
    Includes bibliographical references and index.
    Summary: Explains how, why, when, and where people
    get bullied as well as who does the bullying and what
    can be done about it.
    ISBN 0-8172-5535-4
    1. Bullying—Prevention—Juvenile literature.
    [1. Bullying. 2. Bullies.]
    I. Title. II. Series.
    LB3013.3.P68   1999
    371.58—dc21   97-18226

Printed in Italy. Bound in the United States.
1 2 3 4 5 6 7 8 9 0 03 02 01 00 99

Picture acknowledgments
All photographs by Martyn F. Chillmaid.

Contents

What Is Bullying?

Shouting at someone—that's bullying.

Calling people names—that's bullying.

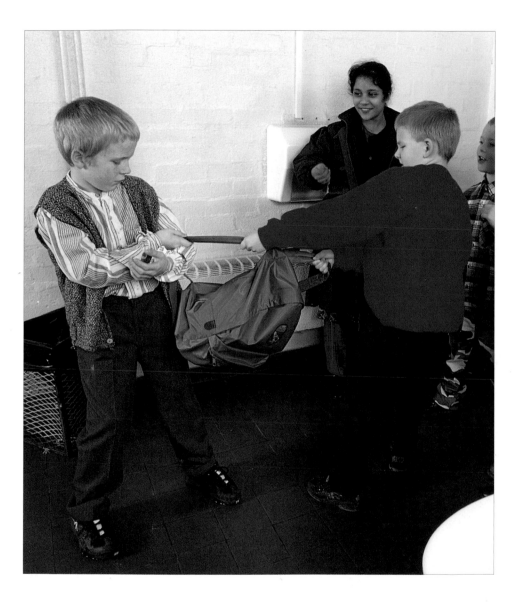

Talking behind someone's back, taking or spoiling their things, hitting or pushing someone around, touching them in a way that makes them feel afraid or unhappy —these are all examples of bullying.

What Is a Bully?

A bully can be a girl, a boy, or an adult.

Anyone who tries to hurt
or upset someone, or make
him or her feel small or
unhappy, is a bully.

There are bullies
at school and
bullies at home.

What Do Bullies Want?

Bullies want to feel big and important.

They want to feel that they are better than other people.

They want to hurt other people and make them feel small.

That's why getting upset or even crying lets bullies have what they want.

Who Gets Bullied?

Anyone can get bullied.

People can get bullied for being big or small, rich or poor.

They can be bullied for the way they look or talk.

Bullies often pick on people because
they are different in some way.
But everyone is different.

It is never your fault if you get bullied.

How Do Bullies Feel?

Bullies often feel unhappy inside.
Sometimes they are jealous of others,
so they try to upset them and spoil
their fun.

Sometimes bullies
themselves have
been hurt or bullied.

John's brother bullied him at home. John didn't like being picked on. It made him feel horrible. At school, he picked on smaller children. It made John feel strong and important when people were afraid of him.

How Does It Feel to Be Bullied?

Being bullied can make people feel afraid and lonely, angry, or upset.

Kate felt too afraid to say she was scared of meeting the bullies.

Being bullied gave Kate nightmares.
She found it very hard to get to sleep.
Some nights she didn't sleep at all.

Kate thought that it was her fault that
she was being bullied.

Where Do People Get Bullied?

People get bullied in school corridors, in bathrooms and locker rooms, in the classroom or on the playground, or at home.

Bullies pick places where they can get someone alone, so they won't get caught.

Why Don't People Tell on Bullies?

It can feel scary to tell on a bully.

Karim thought the bullying would get worse if he got the bully into trouble.

Karim thought about telling his teacher,
but he was scared that she would say
it was all his own fault. He was also
afraid that she might tell him to stop
complaining and fight back.

What Makes Bullying Worse?

Bullying gets worse when bullies get away with it.

They get away with it when people are afraid to tell on them.

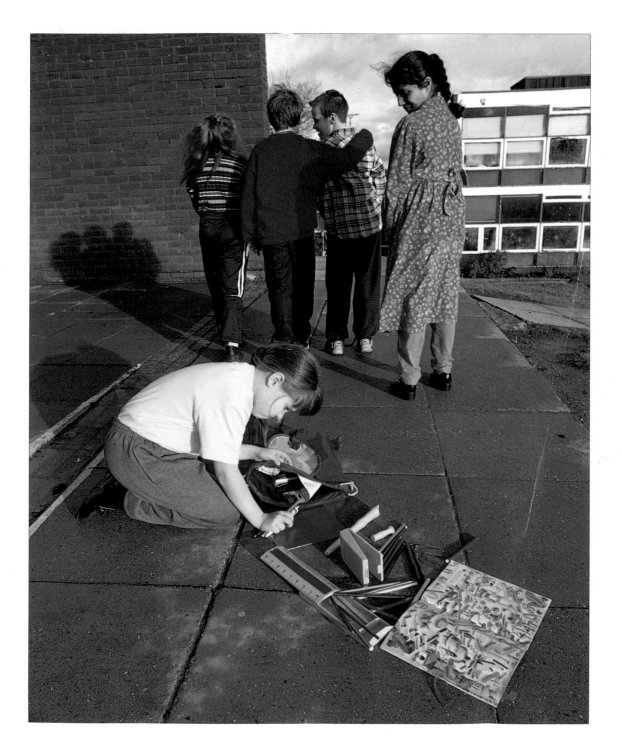

Fighting back can make bullying worse, too.
You can get hurt by fighting a bully.

How Can Bullying Be Stopped?

If someone starts bullying you, try to stay with other people so that the bully can't get you alone.

If a bully tries to make you do something you don't want to do, say "No" firmly and walk away.

If a bully hits or kicks you, try to get away from him or her and get help.

Why Should You Tell on a Bully?

Telling on a bully isn't telling tales.
Bullies must be stopped if they are
making someone else unhappy.
Bullies are also often unhappy, and
they need help.

Clare knew it was important to tell someone about being bullied. The bullies would have kept on bullying if Clare hadn't told her teacher about them. Her teacher said that she could help stop the bullying.

Who Can Help?

If you are being bullied, tell an adult
you can trust. It could be a parent,
someone who cares for you, or a teacher
at school. If this adult won't help you,
find someone who will.

It can help to talk to friends, too. Joining a group or club where you will meet new friends can make you feel stronger and better.

Notes for Parents and Teachers

Use this book as a basis for children's knowledge about bullies and bullying. Ask a group of children why they think people bully. Then ask them how they think bullying makes people feel. Try a role-play situation where a group of children headed by a bully confronts a child. Ask the two characters how they felt during the role-play and work on the feelings they produced.

Mention self-esteem, and how it is important that all children should feel good about themselves and what they do. Ask them about what makes them feel good, such as having fun with your friends. Talk about why having good friends is important, what makes a good friend, and where to make friends (clubs and groups). Happy children do not make bullies and tend not to be bullied.

Talk about the places where people get bullied. Ask the children how they think the places could be made safer. Suggestions could include traveling around in groups and teachers patrolling the corridors and playgrounds.

Talk about who the children can go to, to tell on a bully. Talk about how important it is to tell on a bully and how to make people listen. Emphasize how important it is to tell someone you trust if you are unhappy. Maybe a teacher whom the children trust can be appointed to deal specifically with problems relating to bullying.

Glossary

Jealousy Wanting to have the things someone else has, or to be like them.

Spoil To ruin something or damage it.

Trust When you know someone cares for you and will help you.

Books to Read

Goedecke, Christopher. *Smart Moves: A Kid's Guide to Self-Defense.* New York: Simon and Schuster Juvenile, 1995.

Johnson, Julie. *Bullies and Gangs* (How Do I Feel About). Brookfield, CT: Copper Beech, 1998.

Sanders, Pete and Lacey, Mike. *Bullying* (What Do You Know About). Brookfield, CT: Copper Beech, 1996.

Index

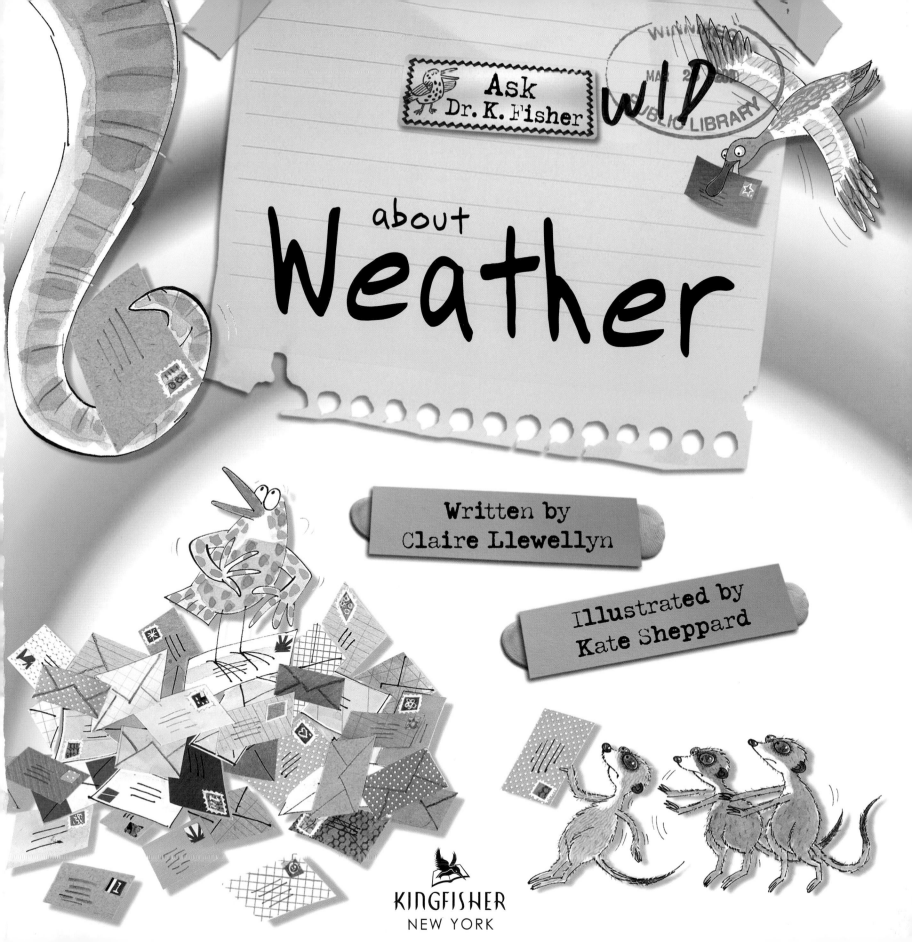

Ask Dr. K. Fisher

about Weather

Written by
Claire Llewellyn

Illustrated by
Kate Sheppard

KINGFISHER
NEW YORK

Claire

Kate

Consultant: David Burnie

Copyright © 2009 by Macmillan Publishers Ltd.
Text and concept © 2009 by Claire Llewellyn
KINGFISHER
Published in the United States by Kingfisher, an imprint of Henry Holt
and Company LLC, 175 Fifth Avenue, New York, New York 10010.
First published in Great Britain by Kingfisher Publications plc, an imprint
of Macmillan Children's Books, London.

Distributed in Canada by H. B. Fenn and Company Ltd.

Library of Congress Cataloging-in-Publication Data
has been applied for

ISBN: 978-0-7534-6254-6

Kingfisher books are available for special promotions and premiums.
For details contact: Director of Special Markets,
Holtzbrinck Publishers.

First American Edition May 2009
Printed in China
10 9 8 7 6 5 4 3 2 1
1TR/0109/MPA/SCHOY/157MA/C

To Dad—our weather man—C.L.
For Richard, our very own
weather man, with love—K.S.

Kingfisher

Henry Holt and Company

175 Fifth Avenue

New York, NY 10010

Ask Dr. K. Fisher about . . . .

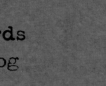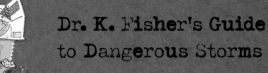
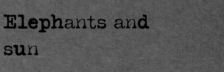

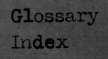

Here's a stork that wants to soar

Stuck on the roof

Dear Dr. K. Fisher,

I'm a young white stork, and I'm worried that I'll never truly fly. I can flap from my nest to the rooftop, but I can't fly up into the sky. I see my mom and dad up there and feel so silly down below. How do they do it? I've tried flapping my wings faster, but they're so long and heavy. Please can you help me?

Losing Heart,
on the rooftop

stork

Dr. K. Fisher
Any problem solved!
1 Diving-in-the-Water
Birdsville 54321

Dear **Losing Heart,**

Don't worry! You will soon be flying high with your mom and dad. Every morning, as the sun warms the land, the air above it gets warmer, too. Warm air is lighter than cold air and rises into the sky. By stretching out your long, broad wings, you storks can ride on the rising air. This will take a little practice, but soon you'll be soaring up into the sky. Trust me—I'm a bird!

All good wishes,

Dr. K. Fisher

Here's a lizard in search of a drink

Water in the air

Dear Dr. K. Fisher,
I'm a lizard, and I live in the desert, where a drink can be difficult to find. Some beetles tell me that they are never thirsty because they find water when they stand on their heads! It's true—I've seen them doing it on the dunes. I've even tried it myself, but I just fall over. Are they crazy?

Feeling Thirsty,
in Namibia

THE DESERT
APR 8TH
MAIL

Dr. K. Fisher
1 Diving-in-the-Water
Birdsville 54321

beetles

6

lizard

Dr. K. Fisher
Any problem solved!
1 Diving-in-the-Water
Birdsville 54321

Dear **Feeling Thirsty,**

Those beetles are on to something—they're getting water from the foggy air. All air contains water, but it's usually an invisible gas called water vapor. Your desert lies near the ocean, and when the air cools at night, a lot of the vapor changes into tiny droplets of water. This creates a thick fog. When the beetles stand on their heads, water collects on their hard, bumpy bodies and runs into their mouths. This won't work for you, but try looking on plants and rocks—you'll find drops of water there.

Best wishes,

Dr. K. Fisher

7

Here's a soggy orangutan

Rain stops play!

Dear Dr. K. Fisher,
I'm a young orangutan,
and I'm feeling fed up. I live
in a tropical rainforest—a great
place to climb and play in the trees.
But every afternoon, when I'm
searching for fruit, it always
pours with rain. Why does
it have to rain so much, and
how can I stay dry?

Grumbler,
in the jungle

frog

hornbills

orangutan

8

Dear **Grumbler,**

Rain's not all bad, you know. It provides us with precious water and helps fruit grow. Rain falls from clouds in the sky. Clouds are made up of billions of water droplets. The droplets bump into one another, getting bigger all the time. When the droplets are too heavy to float, they fall to the ground as rain. Before this happens, the sky grows dark—a warning that you should look for shelter. Also, why not find the biggest leaf around to use as an umbrella?

   Kind regards,

   Dr. K. Fisher

Turn the page for **more about clouds and rain . . .**

9

Dr. K. Fisher's Guide to the Water Cycle

Water plays a big part in the weather. The world's water is always on the move, from the sky to the land and oceans—and then back again. This never-ending journey is called the water cycle, and here is how it works.

5. Rain falls from the clouds.

marmots

owl

ibex

trout

4. Water vapor condenses into clouds.

1. The sun heats the land and oceans.

3. Water vapor rises up into the sky.

eagle

2. Water evaporates from the oceans, lakes, and rivers.

Plants give off water vapor, too.

lobster

6. Rivers carry rainwater to lakes and oceans.

butterfly

11

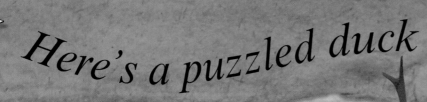

Crash landing

Dear Dr. K. Fisher,

I'm a young duck, and something strange has happened. I flew to the lake as usual this morning, but when I tried to land on the water, I skidded on my behind! The surface was rock solid, slippery, and very cold. I went to warn the other ducks, but worryingly, they've all disappeared. What's going on?

Clueless,
in Canada

moose

duck

Dr. K. Fisher
Any problem solved!
1 Diving-in-the-Water
Birdsville 54321

Dear **Clueless,**

It sounds like winter is on its way. When the weather turns really cold, water freezes into ice—that's what has happened to the surface of your lake. It's difficult for animals to find food during the winter, so some species hibernate until the spring. Ducks do something different: many of them fly away and spend the winter somewhere warmer. This is called migration. It sounds as if your friends have already left, so hurry and catch up with them—they will show you the way.

Happy travels!

Dr. K. Fisher

To the sun

Turn the page for **more about ice and snow . . .**

13

Dr. K. Fisher's Guide to Ice and Snow

When the air is very cold, water droplets inside clouds freeze into solid crystals of ice. These crystals join together and fall as snow, sleet, or hail. Here are the differences between them.

Hail is made inside thunderclouds when ice crystals are whirled up and down. Water vapor freezes onto them and they fall as balls of ice.

Snowflakes are made of ice crystals that stay frozen as they fall to the ground. They are beautiful!

Sleet is a mixture of rain and snow. It is formed when ice crystals start to melt as they fall through warmer air.

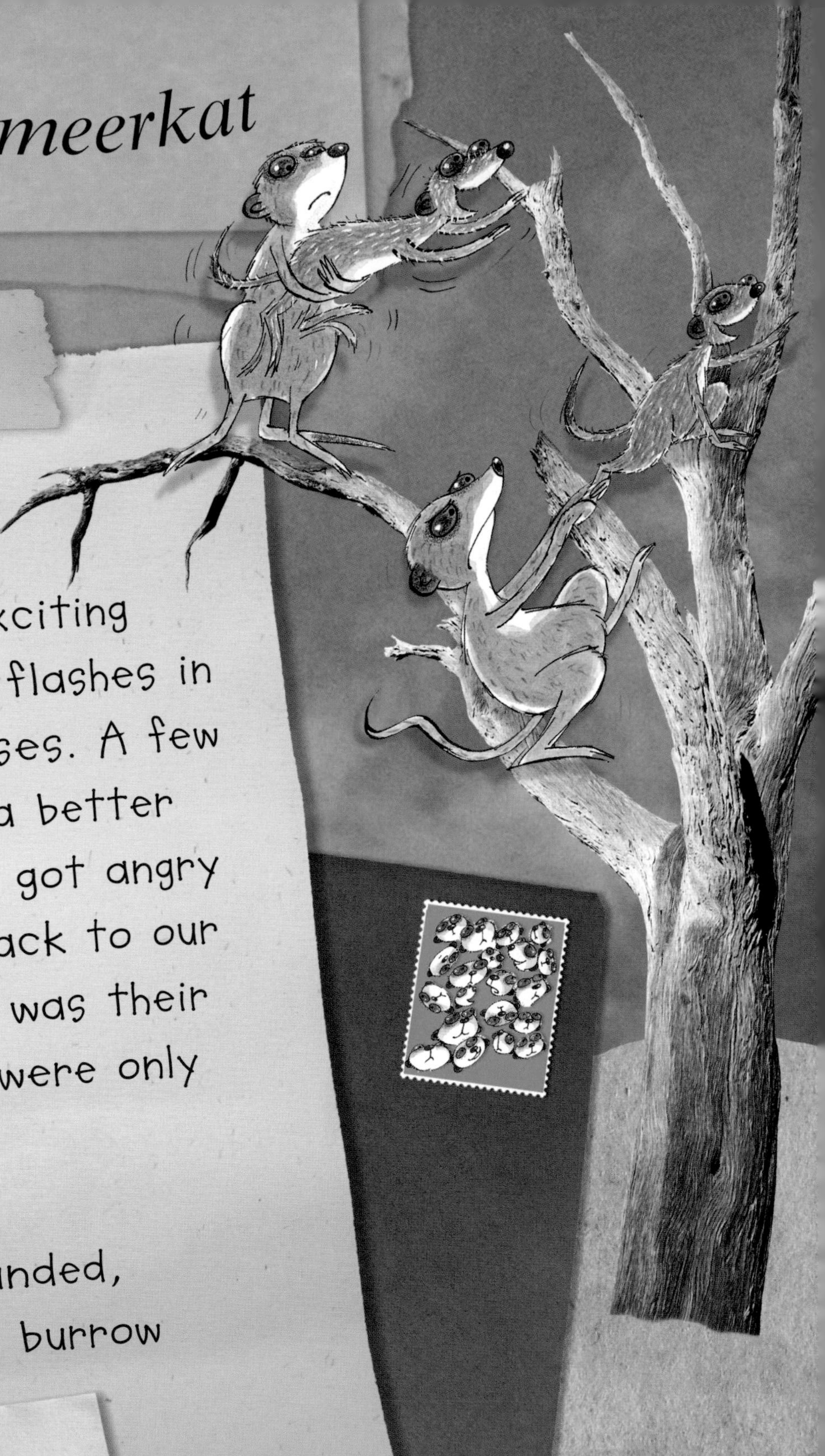

Flashes in the sky

Dear Dr. K. Fisher,

I'm a young meerkat, and the other night something very exciting happened. There were bright flashes in the sky and loud booming noises. A few of us climbed a tree to get a better look, but our moms and dads got angry and sent us back to our burrow. What was their problem? We were only having fun.

Grounded,
in the burrow

meerkat

16

Dr. K. Fisher
Any problem solved!
1 Diving-in-the-Water
Birdsville 54321

Dear **Grounded,**

You saw and heard a thunderstorm. At the end of hot, sticky days, tall thunderclouds often form in the sky. Inside the clouds, strong winds whirl around the water droplets until the clouds crackle with electricity. Sizzling sparks of lightning hit the ground, and the air booms with thunder.

Your mom and dad were being careful. Lightning is dangerous and sometimes strikes trees, so it's best to stay away from them until the storm is over. Your burrow is the very safest place to be.

Warm regards,

Dr. K. Fisher

**meerkats safe
in their burrow**

Here's a giddy trout

Let's twist again

Dear Dr. K. Fisher,
I'm a trout, and I live in a pond. Usually I lead a quiet life, but last week, the most amazing thing happened. My friends and I were sucked out of the water, whizzed around and around in the air, and then dropped back down in the pond. It was mind-blowing! Now, my life seems pretty dull. Do you know how I can do it again?

Thrill seeker,
in the pond

cow

trout

Dr. K. Fisher
Any problem solved!
1 Diving-in-the-Water
Birdsville 54321

Dear **Thrill Seeker**,

No wonder you're feeling unsettled—you've experienced a tornado, one of Earth's most powerful storms! These tall, narrow funnels of air form underneath thunderclouds and spin very fast— so fast that they can rip trees right out of the ground! If a tornado passes over water, it forms a waterspout, sucking frogs and fish high up into the air. You have had a lucky escape. Although they're powerful, tornadoes are small storms, so you're very unlikely to meet one again. Why not enjoy the memory and settle down to life in the pond? It might be quiet, but at least it's safe!

Kind regards,

Dr. K. Fisher

tornado

Dr. K. Fisher's Guide to Dangerous Storms

The most dangerous storms are called hurricanes. This newspaper article tells the stories of three lucky hurricane survivors that lived to tell the tale.

HURRICANE HORROR!
Plucky animals tell their stories . . .

Raging waters

"I was one of the lucky ones," said a crab. "I dug down and sheltered under the mud. Otherwise, I would have been battered by the waves."

Forest drama

"Strong winds tore down the trees," said a tapir, "so I hid in the undergrowth with my calf. Later we crept out to look for food and see what damage had been done."

Blown off course

"I tried to fly out of the storm's path," said a pelican, "but I was blown inland. Now I'm on my way home."

Dr. K. Fisher's Top Tips

★ In a storm, DON'T panic. Think about shelter—can you **hide between** two rocks or **burrow underground?**

★ If the rain is heavy, streams and rivers may flood. DO **move** to **higher, drier ground.**

★ DON'T despair. Remember that **damaged habitats** and **debris can provide new forms of shelter.**

Too much sun!

Dear Dr. K. Fisher,

I'm a young Indian elephant, and I'm baking! Every day, it's sun, sun, sun. Then the next day—more sun! What good does all this sunshine do? And how can I get cool?

Hot and Bothered,
in Bengal

THE FOREST
JULY 31ST
MAIL

Dr. K. Fisher,

1 Diving-in-the water

Birdsville 54321

elephant

monkey

Dr. K. Fisher
Any problem solved!
1 Diving-in-the-Water
Birdsville 54321

Dear **Hot and Bothered,**

Do try and look on the sunny side. The Sun is a ball of superhot gas far away in space, and its rays reach every corner of our planet. You live near the equator, where the Sun's rays are especially strong. Their heat and light help plants grow, providing you and other animals with food all year long. Clouds and rain will return very soon. In the meantime, make your way to a river and cool off in the water.

Yours sincerely,

Dr. K. Fisher

23

Here's a worried snowshoe hare

Snow white

Dear Dr. K. Fisher,
I'm a snowshoe hare, and I'm worried about my fur. Normally, it's a gray-brown color, but now it's started to turn white and there are more white patches every day. I thought this happened only to older animals. Please, Dr. K., I like my brown fur. How can I get it back?

Anxious,
in the Arctic

owl

snowshoe hare

Dr. K. Fisher
Any problem solved!
1 Diving-in-the-Water
Birdsville 54321

Dear **Anxious,**

Don't worry about your fur. It's changing color because the winter is coming and snow is on the way. A white coat will make it difficult for hunters, such as lynx and owls, to spot you on the snowy ground. Your fur grows more thickly now in order to keep you warm. New seasons bring changes in the weather that can affect living things. Your gray-brown fur will grow back again when the warmer days of spring return.

All the best,

Dr. K. Fisher

lynx

Turn the page for **more** about seasons . . . .

25

Dr. K. Fisher's Guide to Seasons

In many parts of the world, there are four seasons every year, and each one brings big changes in the weather. Read this red squirrel's diary to see how her life stays in tune with the seasons.

SPRING

It's spring! The air feels warm and the leaves are sprouting. It's time to build a nest and start a family.

SUMMER

It's hot, but the trees are green and shady. My young kittens find plenty of food to eat. They are growing stronger every day.

Fall has arrived, and the days are cooler. We're getting the nest ready for the winter and eating and storing seeds.

We curl up in the nest on these cold, wintry days. My coat has grown a lot thicker and helps keep me warm.

Dr. K. Fisher's Top Tips

⭐ DO **have** your young in the spring. **This** is the start of the growing season, and there **will be** plenty to eat.

⭐ DO plan **how** to **survive the winter when** food is **difficult** to **find. Will** you **migrate, hibernate,** or **tough** it out?

⭐ If you **decide** to tough it out, DO eat **plenty** in the **fall.** Extra body fat **will help** you **survive.**

27

Here's a fox with the travel bug

climate change

Dear Dr. K. Fisher,
I'm a fennec fox, and I live in the desert, but I love to travel. I'd like to visit my cousin in the Arctic, but my friends say this is a foolish idea and it's too cold for me there. Is this true or are they just spoilsports?

Looking for Adventure,
in the Arabian Desert

fennec fox

Dear **Looking for Adventure,**
I am sorry to disappoint you, but your friends are right. You live near the equator, where the weather is always hot. Your cousin lives near the North Pole, where it is bitterly cold. Your bodies have developed in different ways to cope with these different climates. He has thick body fat, long, warm fur, and tiny ears to stop heat from escaping, while your body is thinner, with very large ears that help keep you cool. I would not advise taking such a hazardous trip. Perhaps you have family closer by?

Kind regards,

Dr. K. Fisher

Arctic fox

North Pole

Arabian Desert

Equator

Arctic fox lives here
Fennec fox lives here

Glossary

air
The mixture of gases that surrounds Earth.

Arctic
The most northerly part of the world, where the weather is very cold.

climate
The weather pattern in a particular part of the world.

condensation
When water vapor cools and changes, or condenses into liquid.

debris
What is left over when something has been broken apart.

equator
An imaginary line that circles Earth at its widest point.

evaporation
When liquid is turned into vapor.

freeze
To turn to ice.

gas
A very light, often invisible, shapeless substance. Air is a mixture of gases.

habitat
The natural home of an animal or plant.

hibernate
To sleep through the winter.

lightning
A gigantic electric spark that leaps out of thunderclouds.

migration
A journey from one place to another at a particular time of year.

rainforest
A thick forest that grows in the warmest, wettest parts of the world.

ray
A beam of light.

season
A part of the year with a particular weather pattern.

thundercloud
A large storm cloud that produces thunder and lightning.

tropical
Describes parts of the world that are found close to the equator, where the weather is always warm.

water cycle
The movement of water between the oceans, the air, and the land.

waterspout
A spinning column of water made by a tornado when it passes over water.

water vapor
An invisible gas that hangs in the air. Water turns into vapor when it evaporates.

Index